A LITTLE BIT OF
Ireland

GILL & MACMILLAN

Contents

Ireland's Patron Saint 10

Dublin 12

'Cockles and Mussels' .16

Pre-Christian Ireland .18

Yellow Man and Soda Bread 20

The Wicklow Mountains 22

Cork 24

'He Wishes for the Cloths of Heaven' 26

Christianity in Ireland 28

Irish Stew 30

The Lakes of Killarney 32

Hurling 34

Limerick 36

The English in Ireland 38

Barm Brack 40

Belfast 42

The Giant's Causeway 44

Gaelic Football 46

Georgian Ireland 48

'The Londonderry Air' ('Danny Boy') 50

Tralee 52

Colcannon & Potato Cakes 54

Famine and the Diaspora 56

Donegal Beaches . . . .˙. 58

Thoroughbred Racing .60

Sligo 62

'The Lake Isle of Innisfree' 64

Modern Ireland 66

Galway 68

Annual Events in Ireland 70

Irish Surnames & Shields 72

Ireland's Patron Saint

Patrick is Ireland's national saint. Traditionally it has been held that he was born about 390, began his mission to Ireland in 432 and died about 461. Many scholars now think that this time frame is about thirty years too early. Clearly he is a rather shadowy figure. All that we know for certain comes from his only two surviving writings, his *Confession* and his *Letter to the Soldiers of Coroticus*. The *Confession* gives us a good idea of his spirituality but has few biographical details. Likewise, the *Letter* attacking the Scottish warlord who slaughtered some of Patrick's new converts and took others into slavery is scant on detail, but gives a picture of him as a dedicated missionary, stern, even fierce in the defence of his flock. Legend has it that Patrick was born in Wales of Roman parents and was captured as a

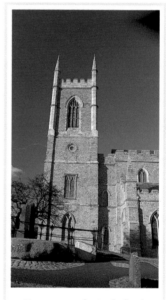

Downpatrick Cathedral

youth in a raid by Irish slavers
and taken to Ulster. In bondage
for six years, he escaped to
Britain, later training to be a
priest in Rome and finally
returning to Ireland to minister
to the Christian Irish there. He
went on to evangelise across the
country, making a great impact
on the pagan society of the time.
The saint was a compelling
character, whose simple faith
and absolute commitment
remain a source of inspiration
today. He is a central figure in
the history of European
Christianity and is recognised
worldwide as the apostle of
Ireland. His feast day on March
17, celebrated on the continent
since the ninth century, is
remembered in every country to
which the Irish have
subsequently emigrated.

Saint Patrick

Dublin

For many, the best of Ireland is embodied in the capital city ·Dublin. Home of an international airport and seaport, it is the seat of the Irish government, headquarters of banks, financial institutions and major international companies, and the hub of great theatres and museums, and yet it exudes a hometown atmosphere, with a friendly pub on every corner. Sitting on the edge of the Irish Sea, straddling both sides of the River Liffey, and rimmed by a semi-circle of inland mountains, Dublin is indeed a 'fair city'.

Ryan's pub

The Four Courts on the River Liffey

Beyond that, the streets are wide and well-swept, parks and pedestrian areas are plentiful, and best of all this compact city is easy to negotiate on foot.

Architecturally Dublin is a good example of a largely intact eighteenth-century Georgian city. The landmark public buildings, sweeping avenues and graceful squares are surrounded by rows of brick-fronted townhouses, each with its own unique door.

A Georgian Dublin door

English is the first language of the Irish. It is often said, in fact, that the best enunciated English in the world is heard in Dublin, especially in literary and scholarly circles. With a recorded history going back a thousand years, at least, Dublin has been home to a roster of citizens as diverse as its own urbane charm – from literary figures such as Jonathan Swift, Oscar Wilde, George Bernard Shaw, William Butler Yeats, Sean O'Casey and James Joyce, to actors such as Gabriel Byrne, rock musician Bob Geldof and international film director Neil Jordan.

The Halfpenny Bridge over the Liffey

'Cockles and Mussels'

In Dublin's fair city
Where the girls are so pretty
I first set my eyes on sweet Molly Malone,
As she wheeled her wheelbarrow
Through streets broad and narrow
Crying 'Cockles and mussels alive, alive, oh!'

CHORUS
Alive, alive oh!
Alive, alive oh!
Crying 'Cockles and mussels, alive, alive, oh!'

She was a fishmonger,
But sure 'twas no wonder,
For so were her father and mother before;
And they both wheeled their barrow,
Through streets broad and narrow,
Crying 'Cockles and mussels, alive, alive, oh!'

CHORUS

She died of a fever
And no one could save her,
And that was the end of sweet Molly Malone,
But her ghost wheels her barrow
Through streets broad and narrow,
Crying 'Cockles and mussels, alive, alive oh!'

Molly Malone's statue in Grafton Street, Dublin

Pre-Christian Ireland

here has been continuous human settlement in Ireland since the end of the Ice Age. The earliest hunter-gatherers probably came from Scotland to the north-east of the island. The oldest known site of human occupation, at Mount Sandel in Co. Derry, has been dated to almost 6000 B.C. Hunter-gatherers were replaced by Stone Age farmers around

Janus Stone, Co. Fermanagh

3500 B.C. They created the first permanent settlements – early agricultural villages – and spectacular burial monuments, of which Newgrange, Co. Meath, is the most celebrated. There had, therefore, been people in Ireland for over 7,000 years

Drombeg Circle, Co. Cork

Newgrange, Co. Meath

before the arrival of the Celts. But this Iron Age people soon swept all before them and by 200 B.C. they had created a uniform culture throughout the whole island. Gaelic was established as the common language, there was a common legal system and a common currency based on the value of cattle. Celtic Ireland was primarily a cattle-rearing society. There was a multitude of petty kingdoms contending with each other, but no strong political centre. Neither were there any towns: the island was wholly pastoral. The Roman Empire never considered the island worth invading, but eventually it was the coming of Christianity, the official religion of the late Empire, which opened Celtic Ireland to the wider world.

Yellow Man

This 'honeycomb' sweet has been associated for centuries with the 'Ould Lammas Fair', which takes place every year at Ballycastle, Co. Antrim. The sweet was traditionally turned onto a slab and kneaded until pale yellow, once cool. It was then chopped into pieces for sale and this is still the way it is sold at the fair to this day.

YIELDS ABOUT 680G/1¹/₂LBS

460g/1lb golden syrup
225g/8oz soft brown sugar
1 tablespoon softened butter
1 tsp baking powder
2 tbsps vinegar

Thoroughly butter a 15-17.5cm/ 6-7-inch square cake tin. Melt the butter in a large saucepan and coat the insides of the saucepan with it. Add the syrup, sugar and finally the vinegar, and stir over a low heat until the sugar and syrup have dissolved. Bring to the boil, then simmer without stirring. Drop a little of the mixture into a cup of cold water – if it sets it is ready. Add the baking powder carefully since it will make the mixture foam. Stir with a long-handled wooden spoon, then pour the mixture into the prepared tin and mark into squares. Break into squares when completely cold.

Soda Bread

460g/1lb plain brown flour
1 tsp salt
1 tsp bicarbonate of soda
1 tsp cream of tartar
1 tsp sugar
280ml/¹/₂ pint buttermilk,
sour milk or fresh milk with
1 tbsp yoghurt

Mix the dry ingredients into a mixing bowl. Mix thoroughly with a round-ended knife, using a lifting motion to aerate. Make a well in the centre and add milk, mixing until the dough leaves the sides of the bowl clean. Knead into a ball, flatten slightly and place on a greased baking sheet. Cut a cross into the top of the loaf. Brush with a little milk and bake in a preheated oven at 200°C/400°F/Gas Mark 6 for 40 minutes. Remove from the oven, turn loaf upside down and return to the oven for a further 5 minutes. The loaf is done when it sounds hollow if tapped on the base. Wrap the bread in a slightly dampened cloth and stand on its side to cool. Cut into quarters, slice and butter generously.

The Wicklow Mountains

isible from most parts of Dublin, the Wicklow Mountains lie to the south of the capital and form its dramatic backdrop. Visitors from the city can reach them in less than an hour and are usually surprised at their wild appearance so soon after the cultured refinements of the metropolis. For the most part, the mountains are inhabited only by sheep; the eye rests on a panorama of rough grazing, lonely waterfalls and small, solitary loughs. Yet for all the air of wilderness, nearby can be found the lavish gardens of Powerscourt mansion, and the peaceful remains of the once-imposing seventh-century monastery at Glendalough.

A distant view of Glendalough's round tower

In the Wicklow Mountains

Cork

Cork is the ebullient metropolis of Ireland's south coast and above all a 'river city'. Even Cork's anthem sings the praises of the river, 'On the Banks of My Own Lovely Lee'. Cork sits between two channels, with a 'mid-town' area that spills over to the north and south river banks. As a result of its unique layout, its relatively remote location, and the plucky attitude of its citizens, the city has asserted its independence from outside authority over the years, earning itself the title of

Town houses in College Road, Cork

Father Mathew Memorial Church and the River Lee

'Rebel Cork'. Corkmen go out of their way to do things their own way, differently from Dublin and the rest of the country, and have even developed their own patois to match the mood of the city, a fast-paced, sing-song, up-and-down way of speaking. It has an almost musical sound to the ears of out-of-towners.

He Wishes for the Cloths of Heaven

Had I the heavens' embroidered cloths,
Enwrought with gold and silver light,
The blue, the dim and the dark cloths
Of night and light and the half-light,
I would spread the cloths under your feet:
But I, being poor, have only my dreams;
I have spread my dreams under your feet;
Tread softly because you tread on my dreams.

W. B. Yeats

Christianity in Ireland

Patrick was not the only Christian missionary in fifth-century Ireland. We know that in 431 Palladius was 'the first bishop to the Irish who believed in Christ', which clearly suggests that Christians were already present on the island even at this early date. It is likely that Patrick was a true missionary, however, preaching the Gospel in pagan Ireland.

The island of Skellig Michael, Co. Kerry

Irish Christianity soon diverged from continental norms. In the social sphere the effect was limited: divorce, for example, remained a secular matter and was still available under the Celts' Brehon Law, while the Irish Church was monastic rather than episcopal. There were no towns to act as foci for diocesan organisation, so monasteries assumed great importance as centres of Christian learning, scholarship and discipline: the monastery at Clonmacnoise, Co. Offaly, was one of Europe's powerhouses of learning. Most of all, the early Irish Church was a missionary Church, reintroducing Christianity to the continent

A page of the Book of Kells

after the Roman collapse. Irish missionaries founded religious settlements all over Europe. Even France and Italy needed to be re-evangelised, while Germanic and Slav lands were brought within the Christian world for the first time.

Irish Stew

There is much argument concerning the authentic Irish stew: the pure tradition uses only mutton, potatoes, onion and seasoning, and this is generally agreed to be the thing.

SERVES 6

2 lb/900 g neck of lamb chops
1 lb/450 g onions
21/2 lb/1.15 kg potatoes
1 oz/30 g butter
2 carrots, chopped
2 celery sticks, chopped
1 large fresh thyme sprig
3/4 pint/425 ml water or lamb stock
white pepper and salt

Chop the onions coarsely. Peel and slice the potatoes thickly. Season the chops well. Put the butter in the bottom of a heavy saucepan and then layer the meat and vegetables, finishing with a layer of potatoes. Bury the thyme in the centre. Pour in the stock or water. Cover the pan tightly with foil and a lid, bring to the boil and then immediately lower the heat and cook gently on the lowest possible heat for about 1^1/$_2$ hours. The meat and vegetables should cook in their juices with very little liquid left at the end, so watch for burning. It may be necessary to add more liquid. Carefully brown the top of the potato under the grill and sprinkle with parsley.

The Lakes of Killarney

Perhaps of all the beauty spots in Ireland, the lakes of Killarney are the best known internationally. There are three principal lakes. The largest is Lough Leane, containing over thirty islands. Muckross Lake is the second largest and the smallest is Upper Lake – both have four islands apiece. Smaller Black Lake and Auger Lake can be seen en route to the Gap of Dunloe. Possessing a timeless beauty, all these are undeveloped and unpolluted. No cottages or trailer parks are permitted along these shores – only lush foliage, such as azaleas, magnolias, hydrangeas and tropical ferns. Cars are not allowed in the parkland, only horse-drawn jaunting cars, the traditional local transport.

The Killarney lakes

Ross Castle, Lough Leane

Hurling

his very ancient Irish sport is reckoned to be the fastest field game in the world. Played between two teams of fifteen-a-side, it is like a very fast form of hockey, except that the sticks have a thick end boss which allows the ball to be lifted. The ball may not be carried by hand for more than a few paces, but may be carried along by balancing it on the boss, a thrilling skill when done at sprinting pace. This game cannot be played defensively. It

Cork and Meath battle it out

Hurling, the fastest field game in the world

is all about passionate, all-out attack in which the ball moves at astonishing speeds. The scoring system is extremely simple to understand. At its best, hurling is as fine a sporting spectacle as can be found anywhere in the world.

Limerick

ituated on the mighty River Shannon, Ireland's longest river, Limerick is rich in fortifications, the most obvious being the impressive thirteenth-century King John's Castle. In many places it is possible to see parts of the old town's defensive walls and

The Treaty Stone

St John's Castle confronts the River Shannon

Georgian town houses in central Limerick

gateways. Although it has had a violent history - Vikings, Normans, Cromwellians and Williamites have all attacked it in the past - today Limerick, the fourth largest city in Ireland, is a proud and peaceful seaport and manufacturing base, rich in Georgian architecture, with a fine gallery, a lively arts centre and a wide variety of shops and cafés.

The English in Ireland

ikings first raided the Irish coast in 795, founded the earliest Irish towns, including Dublin, but never established themselves across the country. The decisive intervention came instead from the Anglo-Normans in 1169. They captured the major towns and much of the fertile countryside. Throughout the Middle Ages, Gaels and Normans vied for control and influence. Many Normans became heavily Gaelicised. Ireland was officially a Lordship of the English crown: effective local control rested with the big Norman magnates. In the early sixteenth century, Henry VIII of England took a more direct interest in the government of Ireland and the Reformation brought a new wave of English colonists. This new Protestant interest was resented by Gaels and Hiberno-Normans alike, most of whom remained Catholic. Wars ensued. The Ulster Gaels were defeated in 1601 and their lands were planted by Anglo-Scots settlers, ancestors of today's Ulster Protestants. In 1649 Cromwell's countrywide campaign broke Catholic resistance and dispossessed huge numbers of landowners, replacing them with English settlers. The Williamite War (1689–91) attempted to undo Cromwell's work but failed. By the early eighteenth century, Ireland was ruled by a Protestant Ascendancy of recent English origin, but the population outside Ulster was still overwhelmingly Catholic.

Trim, Co. Meath, the largest Anglo-Norman castle in Ireland

Barm Brack

he barm brack (barm is the yeasty ferment produced when brewing ale or beer; brack, or breac, refers to its speckled nature) is one of the few Irish traditional breads or cakes raised with yeast, and, like hot cross buns, the origins are lost in antiquity. It is an essential part of the Hallowe'en festivities and usually contains a ring – whoever gets the ring will be married within the year.

> 12 oz/340 g mixed dried fruit and candied peel
> 1¹/4 lb/560 g plain white flour
> 4-5 saffron strands
> 2 tablespoons water
> 1 teaspoon salt
> 2 oz/55 g brown sugar
> 2 teaspoons ground mixed spice, or to taste
> 1 sachet of easy-blend dried yeast
> 3 oz/75 g butter
> 2 eggs, beaten
> ¹/2 pint/280 ml warm milk

To Glaze
> 1 tablespoon sugar
> 4 tablespoons water

Put the saffron to soak in two tablespoons of water for 15 minutes. In a large bowl mix the flour, salt, sugar, spice and dried yeast together. Rub in the butter and then add the fruit and peel. Add the beaten eggs and the saffron mixture to the warm milk. Make a well in the flour mixture and pour in the liquid, reserving a tablespoon. Mix well together, drawing in the flour from the sides. When the mixture will hold together, turn out and knead for 5-6 minutes.

the dough out and knead again briefly; then divide between the cake tins. Press the rings into the centre and allow the dough to rise for a further 30 minutes. Preheat the oven to 220°C/425°F/Gas Mark 7. Brush the cakes with the reserved liquid and bake for about 10 minutes; then reduce heat to 190°C/375°F/Gas Mark 5 and bake until it sounds hollow when the bottom is tapped, about 40-50 minutes. Make a glaze with the tablespoon of sugar and the water, boiled together until reduced. Brush over the bracks and return to the oven to set for 5 minutes.

Return to the bowl and cover with cling film. Allow to rise for about an hour in a warm place. Grease two 8 inch/20 cm cake tins 3 inch/7.5 cm deep and, if you like, wrap two inexpensive rings in greaseproof paper. Turn

Belfast

nce known for its 'Troubles', Belfast today looks forward to a peaceful future. Situated under Cave Hill at the head of Belfast Lough, the city was once Ireland's most industrialised – linen production and shipbuilding being its mainstays. The 'Titanic' was built here, alongside a host of other luxury liners; the Harland and Woolf shipbuilding gantries can still be seen. The River Lagan, upon which the city lies, has been

The Waterfront concert hall

City Hall, a most imposing building, the symbol of Belfast

developed recently to good effect, the Waterfront concert hall being a particularly fine example of new civic architecture. Belfast people are noticeably friendly towards strangers; their character has been described as 'tough on the outside and soft within', and in the main there is greater tolerance towards others than Belfast's history would suggest.

The Giant's Causeway

The Giant's Causeway is a world famous and truly remarkable natural geological formation on the north Antrim coast, lying two miles from the village of Bushmills. Over 37,000 dark basalt columns, most of them perfect hexagonals, are grouped together like honeycombs from the cliff to the shore for about a kilometre. The tallest, known as the Giant's Organ, are about 12 metres high; elsewhere there are strange terraces and shapes that have given rise to other fanciful names, such as the Giant's Horseshoe, the Giant's Loom, the Giant's Coffin and the Fan. The area is designated a World Heritage Site and is associated with stories of the legendary Ulster hero Finn MacCool.

The remarkable Giant's Causeway

44

Gaelic Football

Gaelic football is the most popular spectator sport in Ireland. It was first codified in the 1880s. Unlike hurling, it did not emerge from an old tradition. There was a rough-and-tumble predecessor called 'caid', but its links with the modern game are tenuous. Gaelic football was developed as an Irish alternative to soccer and rugby and contains elements of both. It is played with a round ball which may be caught and handled. High catching is one of the game's more attractive skills. On the other hand, rugby-style tackling is forbidden. The intention of the game is to propel the ball, either by kicking or hand-passing, towards the opponents' goal. The goal posts are H-shaped, like rugby posts. A point is scored if the ball is kicked over the crossbar and a goal (worth three points) if it is sent under the bar past the goalkeeper.

Mayo versus Cork (red)

Powerful play during a Gaelic football match

Georgian Ireland

For almost a century, Ireland was at peace. The elegant squares and streets of Dublin and other towns and many fine country houses reflect the confidence and wealth of the Protestant Ascendancy. But the gap between rulers and ruled was still huge. In the last quarter of the eighteenth century, there was a growing demand for an end to penal legislation against Catholics and Dissenters. In this atmosphere of heightened political tension, the effects of the French Revolution were decisive. Ideas such as republicanism and the Rights of Man fused with older dreams of a Catholic revival assisted by a continental power hostile to England. In the 1790s, this obviously meant France. The revolutionaries of 1798 reflected this mixed inheritance and although their rebellion was defeated, it marked the start of modern Irish nationalism. It also shattered the Georgian idyll. An Act of Union followed in 1800, as the Dublin Ascendancy parliament liquidated itself. The Catholic question grew even more urgent under the leadership of Daniel O'Connell, whose campaign resulted in the passing of the Catholic Emancipation Act of 1829, which finally allowed Catholics to sit in parliament. But O'Connell's campaign to repeal the Act of Union failed.

Left: the Wexford 1798 memorial. Above: Georgian Dublin

The Londonderry Air (Danny Boy)

Oh, Danny Boy, the pipes, the pipes are calling
From glen to glen and down the mountainside.
The summer's gone, and all the roses falling,
It's you, it's you must go and I must bide.
But come ye back when summer's in the meadow,
Or when the valley's hushed and white with snow,
It's I'll be here in sunshine or in shadow,
Oh Danny Boy, oh Danny Boy, I love you so.

But when ye come, and all the flowers are dying,
If I am dead, as dead I well may be,
Ye'll come and find the place where I am lying,
And kneel and say an 'Ave' there for me.
And I shall hear, though soft you tread above me,
And all my grave will warmer, sweeter be,
For you will bend and tell me that you love me,
And I shall sleep in peace until you come to me!

Tralee

The county town of Co. Kerry, Tralee lies close to the Atlantic in the 'beautiful vale of Tralee' and today is the gateway for visitors keen to view the wonderful scenery of the Dingle Peninsula. The town itself is probably best known abroad for the song 'The Rose of Tralee', which has prompted the long-standing 'Rose of Tralee' annual beauty competition. Tralee can also boast one of the most elegant Georgian thoroughfares in the country, an imaginatively recreated medieval Irish community known as 'Geraldine Tralee', and the Siamsa Tire, the national folk theatre of Ireland.

Siamsa Tire, the national folk theatre of Ireland

Flower-bedecked Tralee shops

Colcannon

hough variations of colcannon are eaten all year round, it always forms part of the Hallowe'en table.

SERVES 4

1 lb/450 g kale or green cabbage
1¹/₂ lb/675 g potatoes, unpeeled
1 bunch scallions (spring onions), finely chopped
6 fl oz/175 ml hot cream or milk
4 oz/110 g butter
salt and white pepper

Remove the hard stalks from the kale, or cabbage, and cook in salted, boiling water, until tender. Kale takes a surprisingly long time, about 25 minutes, cabbage will take less. Drain, press out any remaining water and chop finely. Boil the potatoes in salted, boiling water until soft; drain and dry over the heat for a few minutes, covered with a tea-towel. Peel and mash carefully by hand, removing any lumps, but do not use a food processor. Cook the spring onions in the cream or milk for a few minutes. Add them to the potatoes, with the hot cream or milk, half the butter and the kale. Mix thoroughly, check and adjust the seasoning, and put into a large serving bowl. Make a well in the centre, which will hold the remaining butter. Serve very hot.

Potato Cakes

90g/3oz flour
pinch of salt
$^1/_4$ tsp baking powder
20g/ $^3/_4$oz butter
340g/12oz cooked mashed
potato
oil, bacon dripping or butter
for frying

Sift flour, salt and baking
powder into a mixing bowl.
Rub in the butter. Mix in the
potatoes and knead into a ball.
Cut this dough in half and roll
out each piece into a 6mm/$^1/_4$
inch thick circle on a floured
board or work surface. Divide
each cake into 4 segments.
Grease a heavy frying pan with
some oil, bacon dripping or
butter and heat well. Add the
wedges of potato cake and
cook them for 2-3 minutes on
each side.

Famine and the Diaspora

I n the course of his campaigns, Daniel O'Connell had created a mass democracy by mobilising Catholic opinion. Had he succeeded in repealing the Union, the new Dublin parliament would have been different to the Ascendancy-controlled body that disappeared in 1800. Irish Protestants knew this and thus remained Unionist thereafter, fearing Catholic nationalism. O'Connell died in 1847, as Ireland was experiencing the greatest trauma in its history. A famine caused by a mysterious potato blight robbed the population of its staple diet for four years. Two million people, a quarter of the total population, died or emigrated. The response of the British government was niggardly: too little too late. The emigrants, especially those who went to America, took with them a hatred of England that inspired and bankrolled all later nationalist movements in Ireland. The Famine transformed Ireland. The landless cottier class was decimated. The surviving tenant farmers determined that no such crisis would ever recur and a campaign of land reform developed. The ultimate demand was for the transfer of ownership from landlords to tenants. This was accomplished in 1903, effectively reversing the Cromwellian land settlement after some 250 years.

The Famine memorial, Dublin city

Donegal Beaches

Oonegal boasts some of the finest beaches in Europe, many of which have been awarded the EEC's Blue Flag accolade for their high quality. Entirely unspoilt and usually empty, long stretches of golden sand meet the Atlantic in various places along the county's rugged coast and any one of them makes a wonderful place to walk and watch the sun go down. The most famous can be found at Rossnowlagh in the south, Ballymastocker Bay near Portsalon at the mouth of Lough Swilly in the north of the county, Marble Hill and opposite, across Clonmass Bay, Rosapenna Beach to the west.

Ballymastocker Bay

Thoroughbred Racing

The Irish love of horses is world-renowned and the country's place in bloodstock breeding and training is second to none. Given a moist climate to encourage the growth of pasture and an abundance of calcium-rich soil, especially in the south-central part of the country, horses thrive in Ireland. The best can be seen showing off their paces most spectacularly at the Curragh, just outside Kildare, a broad, flat and empty heath which is

STRAINING FOR THE WINNING POST

Ireland's rich soil is ideal for raising fine horses

the setting for all of the great Irish classic races: the Derby, the Oaks, the St Leger and the 2,000 and 1,000 Guineas. For all its glamour, however, flat-racing probably takes second place to steeplechasing in the hearts of most Irishmen, for jump races contain far more unpredictable thrills and spills.

Sligo

Forever associated with Ireland's greatest poet, William Butler Yeats, Sligo is the focus of the Yeats Summer School every August, and numerous hotels, pubs and restaurants are named in his honour. An innovative bronze statue of the poet stands in the centre of the town and not far from Sligo, at Drumcliff, the poet is buried under the shadow of Ben Bulben. Sligo itself has an air

Lough Gill

Town Centre

of genuine unspoilt charm. Swans seem at home on the Garavogue river, which flows down from romantic Lough Gill to the sea. Small, family-run shops with traditional fronts are the norm in the narrow streets and the town can boast a gallery containing a surprising and enthralling collection of Irish paintings, and a ruined 'Abbey'.

The Yeats statue in Sligo town centre

The Lake Isle of Innisfree

I will arise and go now, and go to Innisfree,
And a small cabin build there, of clay and wattles made:
Nine bean rows will I have there, a hive for the honey-bee,
And live alone in the bee-loud glade.

And I shall have some peace there, for peace comes dropping slow,
Dropping from the veils of the morning to where the cricket sings;
There midnight's all a glimmer, and noon a purple glow,
And evening full of the linnet's wings.

I will arise and go now, for always night and day
I hear lake water lapping with low sounds by the shore;
While I stand on the roadway, or on the pavements grey,
I hear it in the deep heart's core.

W. B. Yeats

Modern Ireland

aniel O'Connell's successor as Irish nationalist leader was Charles Stewart Parnell, who succeeded in building a disciplined parliamentary party in the 1880s. Its demand for home rule (domestic autonomy) looked to have succeeded by 1914. By then, however, the rise of nationalism was mirrored by the equally determined organisation of Irish Unionism, reflecting the opposition of Irish Protestants to any weakening of the British link. Unionism was strongest in Ulster, the most Protestant province, and the only part of Ireland where the industrial revolution had taken hold, tying the regional economy into that of north-west Britain.

Then, at Easter in 1916, a rising of extreme nationalists in Dublin resulted in a week-long fight against British troops. Their demands went well beyond home rule: they proclaimed the Irish Republic. A war of independence followed from 1919-21 which resulted in the British leaving most of Ireland, but remaining in the six north-eastern counties which were strongly unionist. The island was thus partitioned and remains so to this day. The Republic of Ireland is now an independent member state of the European Union. Northern Ireland, with its tragically divided history, has remained an unstable British province containing a nationalist minority of over 40 per cent.

The General Post Office, Dublin, centre of the Easter Rising

Galway

O f all the towns on Ireland's west coast, Galway stands out as the most characteristically Irish, with its narrow streets, medieval arches, alleyways and cobblestones. Situated near the mouth of the Galway River near the northeast corner of Galway Bay, it has always been a great seaport. By the 13th century it was trading regularly with Spain, France and Flanders, as well as with distant Baltic lands. In contrast to the older buildings, Galway boasts one of Ireland's

Galway cathedral at sunset

Waterside shops in Galway

largest religious sites, the Cathedral of Our Lady Assumed into Heaven and St Nicholas, opened in 1965. It stands on the skyline like a mini-version of the Vatican. A landmark of a different sort is the Salmon Weir Bridge. Leaning over this old stone span visitors watch in amazement as a parade of salmon leap into the air as they go up the river to spawn.

Annual Events in Ireland

JANUARY
Five Nations Rugby Internationals begin, Lansdowne Road, Dublin.

FEBRUARY
National Steeplechase, Downpatrick, Co. Down, mid-month
Dublin Film Festival, end of month

MARCH

St Patrick's Day, 17th, parade in Dublin, celebrations at St Patrick's burial place, Downpatrick/Saul, Co. Down
17th Horse Ploughing Match, Ballycastle, Co. Antrim

APRIL
Irish Grand National, Fairyhouse, Co. Meath, Easter Monday

Mullingar International Coarse Fishing Festival, Co. Westmeath, end of month
Punchestown Irish National Hunt Festival, Co. Kildare, end of month

MAY
Cork International Choral Festival (end April, early May), Cork city
North West 200, motorcycle race, Portstewart, Co. Derry, mid-month
An Flea Nua, a festival of traditional Irish music, Ennis, Co. Clare

JUNE
Festival of Music in Great Irish Houses
Bloomsday, 16th, Sandycove, Co. Dublin
Irish Derby, The Curragh, Co. Kildare

JULY

Cobh International Folk Dance
Festival, Co. Cork
Galway Arts Festival, international
status, Galway town
Galway Races, Galway city, late July
or early August

AUGUST

Dublin Horse Show,

RDS Showgrounds, Dublin
Kilkenny Arts Week, Co. Kilkenny,
mid-month, classical music
Yeats International Summer School,
Sligo town
Rose of Tralee Festival, Co. Kerry,
third week

SEPTEMBER

Clarenbridge Oyster Festival,
Co. Galway, second weekend
Waterford International Festival of
Light Opera, Waterford town,
third/fourth week
All Ireland Hurling and Football
Finals at Croke Park, Dublin

OCTOBER

Dublin Theatre Festival,
early Oct
Cork International Film Festival,
Cork city, second week
Wexford Opera Festival, Wexford
town, last week/first week Nov

NOVEMBER

Belfast Festival at Queen's University,
arts festival, last three weeks

DECEMBER

Christmas Racing,
St Stephen's Day (Boxing Day)

Irish Surnames and Shields

AHERN is an anglicisation of Ó hEachthianna, from Eachthiarna, meaning 'lord of horses'. The name originated in the tribe of Brian Boru, the Dál gCais, and has always been associated with their homeland in Co. Clare, but today Aherns are most numerous in counties Waterford and Cork. The arms include three herons in an obvious pun on the name.

BOYLE In Irish, Boyle or O'Boyle is Ó Baoghill, thought to be connected to the Irish geall, meaning 'pledge'. In the Middle Ages the family were powerful, sharing control of the entire northwest of the island with the O'Donnells and the O'Dohertys, and the strongest association of the family is still with Co. Donegal.

BRENNAN derives from the two Irish originals Ó Braonáin and Mac Bránáin. The Mac Bránáin were chiefs of territory in the east of Co. Roscommon, and the majority of the Brennans of north Connacht, counties Mayo, Sligo and Roscommon, descend from them. Ó Braonáin originated in at least four areas: Kilkenny, east Galway, Westmeath and Kerry. Of these the most powerful were Kilkenny. After they lost their land to the English, many became notorious as leaders of outlaw bands.

BURKE The first person of the name Burke to arrive in Ireland was William Fitzadelm de Burgo, a Norman knight from Burgh in Suffolk, who took part in the invasion of 1171 and succeeded Strongbow as Chief Governor. He received the earldom of Ulster, and was granted territory in Connacht. His descendants adopted Gaelic laws and customs more completely that any of the other Norman invaders, and became one of the most important families in the country. According to legend, the arms date from the Crusades.

BYRNE or O'Byrne is from the personal name Bran, meaning 'raven'. It is traced back to the eleventh-century King Bran of Leinster. After the Norman invasion, the O'Byrnes were driven from their homeland in Co. Kildare into south Co. Wicklow in the thirteenth century. They took territory there; even today the majority of Byrnes hail from Wicklow or the surrounding counties.

 CARROLL comes, in the vast majority of cases, from the Irish Ó Cearbhaill, from Cearbhall, a very popular personal name thought to mean 'fierce in battle'. It is widespread today throughout Connacht, Leinster and Munster, reflecting the fact that it arose almost simultaneously as a separate surname in at least six different parts of Ireland.

 CASEY, O'Casey and MacCasey come from the Irish Cathasach, meaning 'vigilant in war', a personal name common in early Ireland. O'Casthasaigh arose as a separate surname in at least five distinct areas, in counties Cork, Dublin, Fermanagh, Limerick and Mayo, with Mac Cathasaigh confined to the Louth/Monaghan area. In medieval times, the Dublin and Fermanagh Caseys were the greatest and most prominent.

DONNELLY is Ó Donnáile in Irish, from Donnáil, a personal name made up of donn, meaning 'brown' and gal, meaning 'bravery'. The original ancestor was Donnail Ó Neill, who died in 876 and was himself a descendant of Eoghan, son of Niall of the Nine Hostages, the fifth-century king who supposedly kidnapped St Patrick to Ireland. Their territory was first in Co. Donegal, but they later moved into Co. Tyrone, where the centre of their power was at Ballydonnelly.

FARRELL As both (O') Farrell and (O') Ferrell, this name in Irish is Fearghail, from the personal name Fearghal, made up of fear, 'man', and gal, 'valour'. The original Fearghal or

Fergal, from whom the family claim descent, was killed at Clontarf in 1014. His great-grandfather Angall gave his name to the territory they possessed, Annally in Co. Longford. The present name of both the county and the town derives from the family.

 FINNEGAN In Irish the surname is Ó Fionnagáin, from Fionnagán, a diminutive of the popular personal name Fionn, meaning 'fairhead'. It arose separately in Roscommon and north-east Galway, and in Monaghan, Cavan and Louth. The majority of modern Finnegans are descended from the Ulster family, and the name is most common in counties Cavan and Monaghan.

 GORMAN In the majority of Irish cases the surname derives from the Irish Mac Gromáin from a diminutive of gorm, meaning 'blue'. The original homeland was in Slievmargy, Co. Laois, but they were dispossessed by the Normans and removed to counties Clare and Monaghan. The

Clare branch became known for their wealth and their patronage of poetry. From Clare they spread to Tipperary.

HICKEY The original Irish for Hickey is Ó hIcidhe, from iceadh, meaning 'healer'. The Hickeys were part of the tribal grouping, the DálgCais, which produced Brian Boru, the High King of Ireland who defeated the Vikings in 1014. This grouping had its territory in the area now part of Co. Clare and north Tipperary, and it is this area with which the Hickeys remain closely identified.

KEARNEY Kearney is widespread in Ireland and has a number of different origins. In the west it originated in Co. Mayo near Moynulla, the territory of the Ó Cearnaigh (from cearnach, meaning 'victorious'), where it has also been anglicised as Carney. A separate family of the same name, but anglicised as (O) Kearney, arose in Clare, and migrated in early times to the area around Cashel in Co. Tipperary.

KELLY comes from the Irish Ó Ceallaigh, based on cellach, which means either 'bright-haired' or 'troublesome'. The name was used as a surname in many places, including Co. Meath, the Antrim/Derry area, Galway/Roscommon and Co. Laois. The greatest of these families are the O'Kellys of Uí Máine, or Hy Many, an old territory taking in east Galway and south Roscommon, also known simply as 'Kelly's Country'. They descend from Máine Mór, a fifth-century chief.

LYNCH is unusual in that it has two completely distinct origins. The first is Norman, from de Lench, possibly derived from a place name now forgotten. The family settled initially in Co. Meath, and a branch then established itself in Galway, where they rapidly became one of the strongest of the 'Tribes of Galway'; one of their number, James Lynch, mayor in 1493, is reputed to have hung his own son for murder when no one else could be found to carry out the sentence.

MAGUIRE comes from the Irish Mag Uidir, meaning 'son of the brown(-haired) one'. In Fermanagh it is the single most numerous name in the county. From the time of their first firm establishment, all the associations of the family have been with Fermanagh. By 1300, they ruled the entire county, and for the next 300 years there were no fewer than fifteen Maguire chieftains of the territory. By 1600, Co. Fermanagh simply belonged to the family.

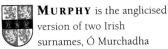

MURPHY is the anglicised version of two Irish surnames, Ó Murchadha and Mac Murchadha, both from the Irish name Murchadh, meaning 'sea warrior'. Mac Murchadha ('son of Murchadh') is exclusive to Ulster. Ó Murchadha (descendant of Murchadh) arose separately in Cork, Roscommon and Wexford. During the 1500s one branch of the family, based in Wexford, retained their lands and their succession continues unbroken today. The arms illustrated are for this family.

NOLAN is the anglicised form of Ó Nualláin, from a diminutive of nuall, meaning 'famous' or 'noble'. The family are strongly linked with an area of Co. Carlow where in pre-Norman times they held power in the barony of Forth. The surname is still linked with the area. There is also a prevalence of the name in Mayo and Galway because a branch of the family migrated there in the sixteenth century and obtained large tracts of land.

O'BRIEN is in Irish Ó Briain, from the personal name Brian. The meaning of this is problematic. It may come from bran meaning 'raven', or, more likely, from Brion, a borrowing from the Celtic containing the element bre, meaning 'hill' or 'high place'. By association, the name would then mean 'lofty' or 'eminent'. The surname itself denotes a descendant of the great Brian Boru (Brian of the Tributes), High King of Ireland and victor at the battle of Clontarf in 1014.

O'KEEFFE and Keeffe are the anglicised versions of the Irish Ó Caoimh from caomh meaning 'kind' or 'gentle'. The original Caomh from whom the family descend lived in the early eleventh century and was a descendant of Art, king of Munster, from 742 to 762. Originally O'Keeffe territory lay along the Blackwater river in Co. Cork but they moved west where their territory became known, and still is known, as Pobal O'Keeffe. The name remains rare outside Cork.

QUINN arose in four areas. In three of these – near Corofin in Co. Clare, in the glens of Antrim, and in Co. Longford – the Irish original from which the name derives is Ó Coinn, from Conn, a personal name meaning 'chief' or 'leader'. The most notable of these families is based in Clare; in early times they were chiefs of the Clan Heffernan, and their descendants are today Earls of Dunraven and Mountearl. The fourth area is Tyrone, where the surname is the county's most common.

RYAN is today one of the commonest surnames in Ireland. Unlike many other common surnames, however, it has one major origin, in the family of Ó Maoilriaghain, meaning 'descendant of a devotee of St Riaghan'. The surname first appears in the fourteenth century in the barony of Owney, on the borders of counties Limerick and Tipperary, where the Ó Maoilriaghain displaced the O'Heffernans. Even today the name is highly concentrated in this area.

SWEENEY comes from the Irish Mac Suibhne, from suibhne, meaning 'pleasant'. The original Suibhne was a Scottish chief based in Argyle around the year 1200. His people were of mixed Viking and Irish descent, and as fighters they were much in demand as mercenaries. Suibhne's great-great-grandson settled in Co. Donegal in the 1300s, but members of his family also made their way to Cork. The Cork family prospered and today the surname is more numerous there.

WALSH is concentrated in counties Mayo and Galway, in Munster in counties Cork and Waterford, and in Leinster in counties Kilkenny and Wexford. It is a semi-translation of the Irish surname Breathnach, meaning 'British' or 'Welsh', also sometimes anglicised as 'Brannagh'. Unlike most of the other Hiberno-Norman families who trace their ancestry to a small number of individuals, the Walshes have many origins: the name arose in different places for obvious reasons.

WHELAN along with its common variant Phelan, comes from the Irish Ó Faoláin, from a diminutive of faol, 'wolf'. Taken together, the two names come among the fifty most numerous in Ireland. The family originated in the ancient kingdom of Decies, part of the modern county of Waterford, where they were rulers up to the Norman invasion. The best known modern bearer of the name was novelist Seán Ó Faoláin, whose family name was originally Whelan.